AF442501

HOW TO ESCAPE RECESSION

A POWERFUL WAY

MYSTIC GURU

Copyright © Mystic Guru
All Rights Reserved.

This book has been self-published with all reasonable efforts taken to make the material error-free by the author. No part of this book shall be used, reproduced in any manner whatsoever without written permission from the author, except in the case of brief quotations embodied in critical articles and reviews.

The Author of this book is solely responsible and liable for its content including but not limited to the views, representations, descriptions, statements, information, opinions and references ["Content"]. The Content of this book shall not constitute or be construed or deemed to reflect the opinion or expression of the Publisher or Editor. Neither the Publisher nor Editor endorse or approve the Content of this book or guarantee the reliability, accuracy or completeness of the Content published herein and do not make any representations or warranties of any kind, express or implied, including but not limited to the implied warranties of merchantability, fitness for a particular purpose. The Publisher and Editor shall not be liable whatsoever for any errors, omissions, whether such errors or omissions result from negligence, accident, or any other cause or claims for loss or damages of any kind, including without limitation, indirect or consequential loss or damage arising out of use, inability to use, or about the reliability, accuracy or sufficiency of the information contained in this book.

Made with ♥ on the Notion Press Platform
www.notionpress.com

"This book is dedicated to the everyday people who are facing the challenges of a recession. To those who are struggling to make ends meet, to those who are searching for financial stability and security. May this book serve as a guide and a source of hope as you navigate the uncertain waters of a recession. May it empower you with the knowledge and tools needed to escape its grasp and find a path towards a brighter future. This book is for you, the unsung heroes who are determined to persevere and overcome the obstacles that come your way. Keep fighting and never give up on your dreams."

Contents

Contents

Foreword

Dear reader,

In today's constantly changing global economy, the possibility of a recession is always lurking in the background. While the thought of a recession can be frightening, it is important to remember that there are steps that can be taken to minimize its impact on your personal finances.

This book, "How to Escape Recession", is designed for the everyday person who may not have a background in finance or economics. It provides practical, straightforward advice on how to prepare for and navigate through a recession. From building an emergency fund to reducing debt, the authors have covered all the essential topics that can help you weather a financial storm.

Whether you are just starting out in your career or are approaching retirement, the tips and strategies in this book can help you protect your financial security during tough economic times. With clear explanations and real-world examples, this guide will empower you to take control of your finances and minimize the impact of a recession on your life.

So, if you are looking for a comprehensive guide to help you escape the effects of a recession, look no further. This book is the perfect starting point.

CHAPTER ONE

Introduction

The recent economic downturn has left many people feeling uncertain and overwhelmed. If you're struggling to make ends meet, or just want to protect yourself from financial insecurity, this book is for you. "How to Escape Recession" offers practical, actionable advice for anyone looking to weather an economic recession. This book is written for the average person, without using technical or financial jargon. It covers all aspects of personal finance, from reducing debt and increasing income to diversifying investments and building an emergency fund. With a focus on long-term stability, this guide provides a roadmap to financial security and peace of mind, no matter what the economy is doing. Whether you're just starting out or well into your career, this book will help you navigate the ups and downs of the economic cycle. So if you want to protect yourself and your family from the impact of a recession, start reading "How to Escape Recession" today

CHAPTER TWO

Build an emergency fund

In recession, building an emergency fund is a crucial step in securing your financial future. Whether it's a job loss, unexpected medical bills, or a natural disaster, life is full of unexpected events that can disrupt your financial stability. An emergency fund acts as a safety net, providing you with the necessary funds to weather these unexpected events without dipping into your savings or going into debt. This book, "Build an Emergency Fund," is designed to help normal people understand the importance of having an emergency fund and how they can go about creating one.

One of the first things to understand about emergency funds is why they are necessary. The truth is, life is unpredictable, and no matter how well you plan, unexpected events can and will happen. Whether it's a sudden layoff, a medical emergency, or a natural disaster, having an emergency fund can provide you with the peace of mind that you will be able to handle whatever comes your way.

In addition to providing financial stability in times of crisis, an emergency fund can also help you achieve your long-term financial goals. For example, if you have an emergency fund in place, you won't need to dip into your savings to cover unexpected expenses, freeing up those funds to be used for other things, like investing for retirement or buying a home.

So how do you go about building an emergency fund? The first step is to determine how much you need to have in your emergency fund. A general rule of thumb is to have three to six months' worth of living expenses in your emergency fund. This will ensure that you have enough money to cover your basic needs, such as rent or mortgage payments, utilities, food, and other essentials, in the event of a financial crisis.

Once you have determined how much you need in your emergency fund, the next step is to start saving. One of the most effective ways to build an emergency fund is to set aside a portion of your income each month. This can be done automatically by setting up a direct deposit into a dedicated savings account or by manually transferring money into the account each month.

Another strategy to consider is to create a budget and look for areas where you can cut back on your spending. This could include cutting back on non-essential expenses like eating out or reducing your monthly cell phone bill. These small cuts can add up quickly and provide you with additional funds to contribute to your emergency fund.

In addition to cutting back on expenses, you may also want to consider ways to increase your income. This could include taking on a part-time job or freelance work, or selling items you no longer need. Any extra money you earn can be used to build your emergency fund.

It's important to remember that building an emergency fund takes time and patience. Don't be discouraged if it takes a while to reach your goal. Instead, focus on making consistent contributions to your emergency fund each month, and stay committed to your plan.

Finally, it's important to keep your emergency fund accessible, but also protected from potential financial predators. A high-yield savings account is a good option, as it allows you to earn interest on your savings while still keeping your funds accessible in case of an emergency.

In conclusion, building an emergency fund is an essential step in securing your financial future. By setting aside a portion of your income each month, cutting back on expenses, and looking for ways to increase your income, you can create a safety net that will provide you with the peace of mind and financial stability you need in times of crisis. So take the time to build an emergency fund today and secure your financial future for tomorrow.

CHAPTER THREE

Reduce debt

In recession, deducing debt can seem like a daunting task for many people. However, it is a necessary step to achieve financial stability and independence. In this book titled "Reduce Debt", we aim to provide practical and actionable advice for the average person to effectively reduce their debt and improve their financial situation.

One of the first things to consider when reducing debt is creating a budget. Understanding where your money is going is essential to identify areas where you can cut back and allocate more money towards paying off debt. This can include reducing non-essential expenses like dining out, entertainment, and shopping, and prioritizing necessary expenses such as housing, transportation, and food.

Another effective strategy for reducing debt is to focus on paying off high-interest debt first. This means targeting credit card debt, personal loans, and other debts that carry high interest rates. By doing so, you will reduce the amount of interest you pay over time and free up more money to put towards other debts.

Consolidating debt through a personal loan or a balance transfer credit card can also be a helpful option for reducing debt. This allows you to combine multiple high-interest debts into one lower-interest payment, which can save you money on interest and make it easier to keep track of your debt.

In addition to reducing expenses and consolidating debt, it is important to focus on increasing your income. This can be done by working overtime or taking on a side job, as well as considering alternative sources of income such as renting out a room in your home or selling items you no longer need.

It is also important to stay informed and educated about your debt and financial situation. This can be done by regularly reviewing your credit report, reading personal finance books and blogs, and seeking the advice of a financial professional if needed.

Reducing debt can also require a change in mindset and habits. This means avoiding impulsive purchases, living within your means, and avoiding taking on additional debt. Additionally, it is important to maintain a long-term perspective and understand that reducing debt will not happen overnight, but rather it is a slow and steady process.

In conclusion, reducing debt is a critical step towards achieving financial stability and independence. By creating a budget, focusing on high-interest debt, consolidating debt, increasing income, staying informed, and changing habits, the average person can effectively reduce their debt and improve their financial situation. With dedication and persistence, anyone can take control of their debt and achieve their financial goals.

CHAPTER FOUR

Diversify investments

In Recession, diversification is a key principle in investing, and it refers to spreading out investments across different assets to minimize risk and maximize returns. The book "Diversify Investments" aims to educate the general public on the importance of diversification in their investment portfolios and provide practical strategies for achieving it. In this essay, we will delve into the concepts discussed in the book and how they can be applied to the average person's investments.

The Importance of Diversification One of the main arguments put forth by the book is that diversification is essential for reducing investment risk. By investing in a variety of assets, you can spread out the risk and mitigate the impact of any one particular investment underperforming. For example, if a person has invested all of their savings in one stock and that stock takes a dive, their entire portfolio will be negatively impacted. However, if they had diversified their investments into multiple stocks, bonds, and real estate, the loss from one stock would be cushioned by gains in the other assets.

Additionally, diversification can also increase returns over time. By investing in a mix of assets, an investor can take advantage of different market cycles and capitalize on the growth potential of various investments. For example, if the stock market is performing well, a portfolio with a mix of stocks and bonds will benefit from both the growth in stocks and the stability of bonds. Conversely, if the stock market is in a downturn, bonds can provide a cushion and help mitigate losses.

How to Diversify Investments The book provides several strategies for diversifying investments, including the following:

- Asset allocation: This involves dividing an investment portfolio into different asset classes, such as stocks, bonds, real estate, and commodities. The idea is to have a mix of assets that perform differently in different market conditions.
- Geographical diversification: This involves investing in different countries or regions to reduce risk. For example, an investor could invest in both U.S. and European stocks to take advantage of the growth potential in both markets.
- Industry diversification: This involves investing in different industries to reduce the impact of any one industry underperforming. For example, an investor could invest in a mix of technology, healthcare, and consumer goods companies to spread out their risk.
- Individual stock diversification: This involves investing in a mix of individual stocks rather than investing in just one or a few. By investing in multiple stocks, an investor can reduce the impact of any one stock underperforming.
- Dollar-cost averaging: This involves investing a set amount of money into investments on a regular basis, regardless of market conditions. Over time, this can help

average out the purchase price and reduce the impact of market volatility.

In conclusion "Diversify Investments" provides valuable insights into the importance of diversification in investment portfolios and provides practical strategies for achieving it. By applying these principles, the average person can reduce their investment risk, increase their returns, and achieve their long-term financial goals. Whether you are a seasoned investor or just starting out, diversifying your investments is a critical step in building a successful and secure financial future.

CHAPTER FIVE

Cut non-essential expenses

In recession, living within your means is a crucial aspect of personal finance. When faced with financial challenges, one of the first things that people often think of is cutting expenses. However, with so many expenses and so little time, it can be hard to determine which expenses are essential and which can be reduced or eliminated. This guide aims to help normal people understand the importance of cutting non-essential expenses, and provides tips and strategies for doing so in a manageable and sustainable way.

Why Cut Non-Essential Expenses? Cutting non-essential expenses has several benefits. First, it can help you save money. By reducing or eliminating non-essential expenses, you can free up money to use for other things, such as paying off debt, building an emergency fund, or saving for a specific goal.

Second, cutting non-essential expenses can help you simplify your life. When you have fewer expenses, you have less to worry about, and you can focus on what really matters to you. This can lead to a more relaxed and stress-free life.

Finally, cutting non-essential expenses can help you prioritize your spending. When you take a hard look at your expenses, you can see where your money is going and make more informed decisions about how to allocate your resources.

How to Cut Non-Essential Expenses Cutting non-essential expenses requires a combination of discipline, creativity, and determination. Here are some tips and strategies for cutting your expenses:

Make a budget: A budget is an essential tool for tracking your expenses and identifying areas where you can cut back. Start by listing all of your monthly expenses and then categorize them as essential or non-essential.

Identify your biggest expenses: Once you have a list of your expenses, look for areas where you can make significant cuts. For example, you might be spending a lot of money on eating out, entertainment, or subscriptions that you don't really need.

Cut unnecessary subscriptions: Subscriptions can be a big drain on your budget, and many of them can be cut or reduced. For example, you might be able to cancel your cable or streaming service and switch to a cheaper alternative.

Cook at home: Eating out can be a major expense, and cooking at home is often much cheaper. Consider meal planning and grocery shopping to save money and eat healthier.

Reduce entertainment costs: Entertainment can also be a big expense, and there are many ways to enjoy yourself without spending a lot of money. For example, you can watch free movies online, take a hike, or host a potluck dinner.

Shop around: When you need to buy something, take the time to shop around and compare prices. You might be able to find a better deal by looking online or visiting a discount store.

Make do with what you have: Before buying something new, consider whether you can make do with what you already have. For example, you might be able to fix a broken item instead of buying a new one.

Be mindful of impulse purchases: Impulse purchases can add up quickly, so it's important to be mindful of them. Try to wait 24 hours before making a purchase, and ask yourself whether it's really necessary.

Cutting non-essential expenses can be challenging, but it is also one of the most effective ways to improve your financial situation. By following the tips and strategies outlined in this guide, you can reduce your expenses, simplify your life, and prioritize your spending. Remember to be disciplined, creative, and determined,

CHAPTER SIX

Increase income

In today's economy, it's not uncommon for people to struggle with their finances. Rising costs of living, stagnant wages, and an uncertain job market can make it difficult to make ends meet. However, there is hope. By taking a proactive approach to increasing your income, you can improve your financial stability and gain greater control over your future. In this essay, we will explore some strategies that the average person can use to increase their income.

Start by Assessing Your Current Financial Situation

The first step in increasing your income is to assess your current financial situation. This includes understanding your income, expenses, debts, and savings. Create a budget that details your monthly expenses, including necessities such as rent or mortgage payments, utilities, food, transportation, and insurance. Be sure to account for discretionary spending, too, such as entertainment, dining out, and shopping. Once you have a clear understanding of your financial situation, you can start looking for ways to increase your income.

Get a Side Hustle

A side hustle is a part-time job or freelance gig that you can do on the side of your regular job. There are many opportunities for side hustles today, including online tutoring, pet-sitting, house cleaning, or delivery services. You can also consider starting your own small business, such as selling handmade items online or providing a service such as photography or home repair. By finding a side hustle that fits your interests and skills, you can increase your income while enjoying what you do.

Negotiate Your Salary

Another way to increase your income is to negotiate your salary at your current job. This can be a bit nerve-wracking, but it's worth the effort if you can get a raise. Before you ask for a raise, research the average salary for your job and the industry in which you work. Prepare a list of your accomplishments and the value you bring to the company. Then, schedule a meeting with your manager to discuss your compensation. Be confident and professional, and have a specific number in mind when you make your request. If your employer can't offer you a raise, you can also ask for additional benefits, such as more time off or flexible scheduling.

Improve Your Skills

Another way to increase your income is to improve your skills. This could mean getting a certification in your field, taking courses to learn new skills, or volunteering for projects at work. By improving your skills, you can become more valuable to your employer and increase your chances of getting a raise or finding a better-paying job. Additionally, investing in your education can increase your earning potential over the long-term.

Explore Freelance Opportunities

Freelancing is another way to increase your income. If you have a skill, such as writing, graphic design, or programming, you can offer your services on freelance platforms, such as Upwork or Fiverr. You can also reach out to friends, family, or local businesses to offer your services. Freelancing allows you to work on your own terms, set your own rates, and have the flexibility to take on as many or as few projects as you like.

Reduce Your Expenses

Finally, reducing your expenses is an effective way to increase your income. By cutting unnecessary expenses, such as cable TV or eating out, you can free up more money to put toward increasing your income or saving for the future. Additionally, consider making changes to your lifestyle, such as downsizing your home, carpooling, or taking public transportation. By reducing your expenses, you can increase your income and improve your financial stability.

Increasing your income is a powerful way

CHAPTER SEVEN

Stay informed

Recession is a period of economic downturn characterized by decreased production, increased unemployment, and decreased consumer spending. This can be a challenging time for individuals and businesses alike. However, staying informed about current events and the stock market can help individuals to better understand the impact of the recession and make informed decisions about their finances.

It is important for individuals to keep abreast of current events during a recession. This includes news about the economy, the job market, and the stock market. By staying informed, individuals can have a better understanding of the causes and effects of the recession, as well as any potential solutions that may be proposed by government or financial experts. For example, if a government announces a stimulus package aimed at boosting the economy, individuals can understand the implications of this package on their personal finances and take advantage of any opportunities that may be available to them.

In addition to staying informed about current events, individuals should also stay informed about the stock market. During a recession, stock prices may be volatile, but understanding the market and its trends can help individuals to make informed decisions about their investments. It is important to remember that while stock prices may fluctuate in the short term, the stock market has a historical tendency to recover over the long term. As such, it is often advised that individuals maintain a long-term perspective and not make hasty investment decisions based on short-term market fluctuations.

Individuals should also consider sharing information about the current state of the economy and the stock market with friends, family, and colleagues. This can be done through word of mouth, through social media, or by participating in community events or financial literacy programs. Sharing information can help to educate and empower others, and can also serve as a source of comfort and support during a challenging time.

When it comes to making informed decisions about personal finances during a recession, there are a number of steps that individuals can take. One of the most important is to build an emergency fund. This fund should be enough to cover at least three to six months' worth of living expenses in case of unexpected job loss or other financial emergency. In addition, individuals should strive to reduce their debt and prioritize savings over non-essential expenses.

Another important step during a recession is to diversify investments. This can help to reduce the impact of market fluctuations and ensure that individuals have a mix of investments that are less vulnerable to economic downturns. Additionally, individuals should consider alternative investments, such as real estate, which may offer a more stable return during a recession.

Finally, individuals should also be proactive about their job security during a recession. This may involve improving skills and education, networking for job opportunities, or considering starting a business. In addition, individuals should be open to new job opportunities, even if they are outside their comfort zone, and be adaptable in their job search.

In conclusion, staying informed about current events and the stock market during a recession is crucial for individuals to understand the impact of the economic downturn on their personal finances. By staying informed, sharing information with others, and taking proactive steps to manage their finances, individuals can mitigate the impact of the recession and maintain financial stability during this challenging time.

CHAPTER EIGHT

Maintain a long-term perspective

During the time of recession, it is important to maintain a long-term perspective on current events and the stock market in order to accurately calculate the impact of a recession.

One of the most important things to do during a recession is to not panic. Panic selling of stocks during a recession can cause a vicious cycle of further economic decline. Instead, it is important to take a step back and consider the long-term perspective. Historically, recessions have always been followed by periods of economic growth. This means that even if the stock market and economy appear to be struggling now, it is likely that there will be a period of recovery in the future.

Another important aspect to consider during a recession is to diversify investments. Diversification helps to spread out risk across multiple investments, reducing the impact of any one investment's performance. This is particularly important during a recession, as certain industries may be more heavily affected than others. By diversifying investments, an individual can ensure that their portfolio is not overly exposed to any one industry or sector.

It is also important to reduce debt during a recession. This will help to free up funds that can be used for essential expenses, as well as giving individuals a financial cushion during periods of economic uncertainty. This can be achieved through various methods such as paying off high-interest debt, negotiating better payment terms with creditors, and finding ways to increase income.

In addition to reducing debt, it is important to focus on necessities during a recession. This means cutting non-essential expenses and prioritizing spending on necessities such as housing, food, and healthcare. This will help to free up funds that can be used for savings and investment, as well as reducing financial stress during a time of economic uncertainty.

Another important strategy during a recession is to take advantage of lower prices. This may mean purchasing items that were previously too expensive, or taking advantage of discounted prices on investments such as stocks. This can help individuals to build their wealth over the long-term, even during a period of economic slowdown.

Finally, it is important to seek advice from financial experts during a recession. This can help individuals to make informed decisions about their investments and finances, as well as to understand the long-term impact of a recession on their financial future.

In conclusion, it is important to maintain a long-term perspective on current events and the stock market during a recession in order to accurately calculate the impact. This may involve reducing debt, diversifying investments, focusing on necessities, taking advantage of lower prices, and seeking advice from financial experts. By following these strategies, individuals can help to protect their financial future and ensure that they are able to weather the impact of a recession.

CHAPTER NINE

The impact of a recession can be felt throughout society, causing people to feel anxious and worried about their financial future. While it is natural to be concerned about the impact of a recession, it is important to understand that panicking is not a productive response. Instead, it is important to approach the situation with a calm and measured understanding of the facts.

One of the biggest concerns during a recession is the impact of current events on the stock market. The stock market is a barometer of the overall health of the economy, and when economic activity slows, it can lead to a drop in stock prices. This can be a frightening experience for those who have invested their savings in the stock market, and it can lead to a feeling of helplessness. However, it is important to remember that stock market fluctuations are a normal part of the economic cycle and that prices tend to recover over time.

It is also important to understand that current events can have a significant impact on the stock market. For example, political events such as elections or international tensions can cause significant fluctuations in stock prices. While these events may feel outside of our control, it is important to keep a long-term perspective and remember that the stock market has a tendency to bounce back over time.

In order to calculate the impact of a recession on the stock market, it is important to understand the underlying factors that are driving the economy. For example, the unemployment rate, consumer spending, and the performance of key industries are all important indicators of the health of the economy. When these factors start to decline, it can indicate that a recession is on the horizon, which can lead to a decrease in stock prices.

However, it is important to remember that the stock market is a forward-looking indicator and that it tends to anticipate future economic activity. This means that a drop in stock prices can actually be a sign that the economy is about to recover, and that prices will eventually start to rise again.

In addition to understanding the impact of current events and the stock market, it is also important to take a calm and measured approach to our own finances during a recession. This means avoiding hasty financial decisions, such as selling all of our investments, and focusing instead on developing a long-term financial plan.

One of the best ways to minimize the impact of a recession is to build an emergency fund. This fund should be used to cover essential expenses such as food, housing, and transportation, in the event that you lose your job or experience a reduction in income. This will help you to maintain your standard of living and reduce the stress that comes with financial uncertainty.

Another key strategy for minimizing the impact of a recession is to reduce debt. This means paying off credit card balances, student loans, and other forms of high-interest debt, which can be especially burdensome during a period of economic uncertainty.

Diversifying your investments is another important strategy for minimizing the impact of a recession. This means spreading your investments across different asset classes, such as stocks, bonds, and real estate, so that you are not overly exposed to any one sector of the economy. This can help to reduce your overall risk and provide a greater degree of stability during a period of economic uncertainty.

It is also important to cut non-essential expenses during a recession, in order to free up money for savings and investment. This can include cutting back on dining out, entertainment, and travel, as well as reducing your overall spending on luxury items.

CHAPTER TEN

Keep a stable work schedule

A recession can bring a great deal of uncertainty and insecurity to people's lives, especially when it comes to their work and financial situation. During a recession, unemployment rates tend to rise, and many people find themselves struggling to keep their job or find a new one. It is therefore essential to adopt a strategy that will help you maintain your job security and stability, even during tough economic times.

One of the best ways to achieve this stability is to keep a stable work schedule during a recession. This means staying focused on your job and continuing to work as hard as you normally would, even if the economic conditions are challenging. This is important for several reasons.

First, keeping a stable work schedule can help you maintain your job security. During a recession, many businesses are looking for ways to cut costs, and one of the first things they often do is lay off workers. However, if you are seen as a valuable and reliable employee, your boss is less likely to let you go, even during a tough economic climate. By keeping a stable work schedule, you can demonstrate your commitment to your job and your employer, and make yourself a less attractive target for layoffs.

Second, keeping a stable work schedule can help you maintain your income. During a recession, many people find themselves struggling to make ends meet, and their financial situation can become increasingly uncertain. By keeping your job and continuing to earn a steady income, you can help ensure that you have the resources you need to pay your bills and support your family, even during tough times.

Third, keeping a stable work schedule can help you build your skills and experience. This is particularly important during a recession, as it can be difficult to find new job opportunities. By focusing on your current job and working hard to develop your skills, you can position yourself to be a more competitive candidate when the economy recovers and new job opportunities become available.

There are several things you can do to keep a stable work schedule during a recession. First, it is important to stay focused on your job and continue to work as hard as you normally would, even if the economic conditions are challenging. This means avoiding distractions, such as checking your phone or social media, and putting in the effort to complete your work to the best of your ability.

Second, it is important to communicate with your employer about your work schedule and availability. This will help you ensure that your employer understands your commitment to your job, and can help to avoid any misunderstandings or miscommunications that could affect your job security.

Third, it is important to be proactive about seeking out new job opportunities, even if you are currently employed. This means networking with others in your industry, attending job fairs and workshops, and exploring new job opportunities that may be available. This can help you stay on top of changes in the job market and ensure that you are well-positioned to take advantage of new job opportunities when they become available.

Finally, it is important to maintain a positive attitude and focus on your goals, even during tough times. This means staying motivated and driven, even when the economic conditions are challenging, and continuing to pursue your goals and aspirations. By doing so, you can help ensure that you are well-positioned to succeed, even during tough economic times.

In conclusion, keeping a stable work schedule during a recession is essential for maintaining job security, income, and financial stability. By focusing on your job, communicating with your employer, being proactive about job opportunities, and maintaining a positive attitude, you can help ensure that you are well-positioned to weather the economic storm and emerge stronger on the other side.

Avoid big purchases

There are steps that individuals can take to minimize the impact of a recession on their financial well-being. One of the most effective ways to do this is by avoiding big purchases during a recession.

The importance of avoiding big purchases during a recession lies in the fact that, when economic activity slows, it can be more difficult to find work or to keep your current job. This can lead to a decrease in income and an increase in financial uncertainty, making it difficult to make ends meet. By avoiding big purchases, you can reduce your overall expenses and increase your savings, which will help you to weather the economic storm and maintain your financial stability.

One of the most important things to consider when avoiding big purchases during a recession is timing. If you are already facing financial difficulties or if you expect to lose your job, it is especially important to avoid making any large purchases that will put additional strain on your finances. This may mean putting off a home renovation project or delaying the purchase of a new car.

Another important factor to consider when avoiding big purchases during a recession is the type of purchase. While it may be tempting to buy a big-ticket item such as a luxury car or an expensive piece of jewelry, these purchases can be particularly damaging during a recession, when you are more likely to experience financial uncertainty. Instead, focus on necessities, such as food, housing, and transportation, and avoid making any purchases that are not essential to your daily life.

In addition to considering timing and type, it is also important to consider the cost of the purchase. Large purchases often come with a high price tag, and they can also involve additional costs, such as interest payments and maintenance expenses. By avoiding big purchases, you can reduce your overall expenses and free up money for other important expenses, such as saving for the future or paying off debt.

So, how can you avoid big purchases during a recession? One of the best ways is to create a budget. A budget can help you to track your spending and identify areas where you can cut back. By reducing your overall expenses, you can free up money for savings and investment, which will help you to weather the economic storm and maintain your financial stability.

Another key strategy for avoiding big purchases during a recession is to focus on necessities. This means prioritizing your spending on essential items, such as food, housing, and transportation, and avoiding non-essential purchases, such as luxury items or entertainment expenses.

It is also important to be proactive about job security during a recession. This may mean seeking advice from a financial expert, improving your skills and education, or networking for job opportunities. By being proactive, you can increase your chances of maintaining your income and reduce the risk of financial uncertainty.

Finally, it is important to seek support from loved ones during a recession. This can be a difficult and stressful time, and having a support system can help you to stay motivated and maintain a positive outlook.

In conclusion, avoiding big purchases during a recession is a key strategy for minimizing the impact of a recession on your financial well-being. By considering timing, type, and cost, and focusing on necessities and job security, you can reduce your expenses and increase your savings, which will help you to weather the economic storm and maintain your financial stability.

CHAPTER TWELVE

Keep investment portfolios balanced

A recession can be a challenging time for investors, as it often leads to a decline in stock prices and economic activity. However, with a calm and measured approach, it is possible to minimize the impact of a recession on your investment portfolio. One of the key strategies for doing so is to maintain a balanced portfolio, which can help to reduce your overall risk and provide a greater degree of stability during this uncertain time.

Balancing your investment portfolio means spreading your investments across different asset classes, such as stocks, bonds, and real estate. This helps to reduce your overall risk, as different types of investments perform differently during different stages of the economic cycle. For example, while stocks tend to perform well during periods of economic growth, they can be volatile during a recession. On the other hand, bonds tend to be more stable and can provide a steady source of income during a period of economic uncertainty.

Another important aspect of maintaining a balanced portfolio is to diversify your investments within each asset class. This means investing in a range of stocks, bonds, and real estate properties, instead of putting all your money into one or two investments. This helps to reduce your exposure to any one company or sector, and can help to protect your portfolio in the event of a market downturn.

In addition to balancing your portfolio, it is also important to maintain a long-term perspective during a recession. This means avoiding the temptation to panic and sell your investments when the market experiences a decline. Instead, it is important to focus on your long-term goals and to remember that the stock market has a tendency to recover over time.

One of the biggest challenges during a recession is to manage your emotions and avoid making hasty financial decisions. This can be especially difficult when the stock market is experiencing significant declines and the news is filled with negative headlines. However, it is important to keep a level head and to avoid making decisions based on fear or panic.

If you are feeling anxious or worried about your investments during a recession, it may be helpful to seek the advice of a financial professional. A financial advisor can provide you with a more objective perspective on your investments and help you to make informed decisions based on your specific financial situation and goals.

Another important strategy for managing your investments during a recession is to consider alternative investments, such as real estate or commodities. These investments can provide diversification and can help to reduce your overall risk, as they tend to perform differently than stocks and bonds during different stages of the economic cycle.

It is also important to focus on the fundamentals of your investments, such as the financial performance of the companies in which you have invested. This can help you to identify which investments are likely to perform well during a recession, and which ones may be more vulnerable to market fluctuations.

Finally, it is important to stay informed about the economic situation and to be proactive about managing your investments. This means monitoring your portfolio regularly, adjusting your investments as needed, and taking advantage of opportunities to buy high-quality investments at lower prices.

In conclusion, a balanced investment portfolio and a long-term perspective are key strategies for minimizing the impact of a recession on your investments. By diversifying your investments, seeking professional advice, and staying informed about the economic situation, you can help to protect your portfolio and achieve your long-term financial goals.

CHAPTER THIRTEEN

Consider alternative investments

Recession is a normal part of the economic cycle, characterized by a period of declining economic activity, which can lead to higher unemployment and reduced consumer spending. While this can be a stressful time for investors, it is also an opportunity to explore alternative investments that can help to mitigate the impact of the recession.

One of the first things to consider during a recession is the safety of your current investments. For example, if you have a large portion of your portfolio invested in the stock market, it may be wise to consider rebalancing your portfolio to include a greater proportion of bonds or other fixed-income assets. These types of investments are generally considered to be less risky and can provide a greater degree of stability during a period of economic uncertainty.

Another alternative investment to consider during a recession is real estate. While the real estate market can also be impacted by economic downturns, it has been shown to be a relatively stable investment over the long-term. Furthermore, real estate investments can provide a steady stream of income through rental income, which can be especially valuable during a period of high unemployment.

If you are considering investing in real estate, it is important to understand the local real estate market and to have a clear investment strategy in place. This may include investing in rental properties, flipping homes, or investing in real estate investment trusts (REITs). Each of these options has its own advantages and disadvantages, and it is important to research and consider your options carefully before making a decision.

Another alternative investment to consider during a recession is commodities, such as gold or silver. Commodities are often seen as a hedge against inflation and economic uncertainty, and they have the potential to provide a stable return during a period of declining economic activity. However, it is important to understand the risks associated with commodity investing, and to seek professional advice if you are considering this type of investment.

For those who are looking for a more hands-off approach to alternative investing, exchange-traded funds (ETFs) can be a good option. ETFs are investment funds that track a specific market or sector, and they can provide exposure to a diverse range of assets, including commodities, real estate, and bonds. This can help to reduce the overall risk of your portfolio and provide a greater degree of stability during a period of economic uncertainty.

Finally, it is important to understand that alternative investments are not a guaranteed way to protect your portfolio during a recession. As with any type of investment, there are risks involved, and it is important to consider your overall financial situation and risk tolerance before making any investment decisions.

In conclusion, considering alternative investments during a recession can help to mitigate the impact of declining economic activity and provide a greater degree of stability for your portfolio. However, it is important to understand the risks involved, to seek professional advice, and to have a clear investment strategy in place before making any investment decisions. By taking a calm and measured approach to alternative investing during a recession, you can help to ensure the long-term health and growth of your portfolio, no matter what the economic conditions may be.

CHAPTER FOURTEEN

Consider part-time work

A recession leads to job losses, reduced consumer spending, and economic uncertainty. However, it is important to remember that recessions are a normal part of the economic cycle, and that they will eventually pass. While it can be tempting to panic and give up hope, there are many strategies that people can use to minimize the impact of a recession and improve their financial situation. One of these strategies is to consider part-time work during a recession.

Part-time work can offer many benefits during a period of economic uncertainty. For example, it can provide a source of income to help you make ends meet, even if you have lost your full-time job. Part-time work can also help you to build your skills and experience, which can increase your employability and make it easier for you to find a full-time job in the future.

Part-time work is also a great way to supplement your income during a recession. This can be especially helpful if you have experienced a reduction in your full-time income, or if you are looking for ways to increase your overall financial stability. With part-time work, you can earn extra money to help cover your bills, build your savings, and invest in your future.

In addition to the financial benefits of part-time work, there are also many other advantages. For example, part-time work can offer greater flexibility and independence, allowing you to balance your work with other commitments and interests. This can be especially helpful if you are looking for ways to reduce your stress and improve your quality of life during a period of economic uncertainty.

When considering part-time work during a recession, it is important to consider your skills, experience, and interests. This will help you to find a part-time job that is a good fit for you and that will allow you to make the most of your abilities.

One of the best ways to find part-time work is to network with friends, family, and colleagues. You may be surprised to find that someone you know has a part-time job opportunity that is perfect for you. In addition, you can also search online job boards, local classifieds, and community centers for part-time job opportunities in your area.

Another important factor to consider when looking for part-time work during a recession is the type of work you are looking for. For example, you may want to look for part-time jobs that are in your field of expertise, as this will allow you to build your skills and experience in your chosen area. Alternatively, you may want to consider part-time work in a different field that interests you, as this can help you to expand your horizons and gain new experiences.

When applying for part-time work, it is important to be professional and prepare a strong resume and cover letter.

You should also be prepared to attend job interviews, as this will allow you to demonstrate your skills and enthusiasm for the position.

In conclusion, considering part-time work during a recession can be a smart and effective way to minimize the impact of economic uncertainty and improve your financial situation. By finding a part-time job that is a good fit for your skills, experience, and interests, you can gain valuable work experience, supplement your income, and improve your overall financial stability. So, if you are looking for ways to cope with the challenges of a recession, consider part-time work as a smart and effective solution.

CHAPTER FIFTEEN

Prioritize savings

The impact of a recession can be felt throughout society, causing people to feel anxious and worried about their financial future. In these uncertain times, it is important to prioritize savings in order to minimize the impact of a recession and ensure a stable financial future.

One of the biggest impacts of a recession is the increase in unemployment. When people lose their jobs, their income is reduced, making it more difficult to pay bills and maintain their standard of living. During a recession, it is important to have a strong savings account that can be used to cover essential expenses and help you to weather the storm of unemployment.

Prioritizing savings also means being mindful of your spending and making smart financial decisions. This includes cutting back on non-essential expenses and reducing your overall spending on luxury items. By reducing your expenses, you can free up money for savings and investment, which can help you to weather the economic uncertainty of a recession.

In order to prioritize savings during a recession, it is important to create a budget and stick to it. This means tracking your spending and identifying areas where you can cut back. This can include reducing your overall spending on dining out, entertainment, and travel, as well as cutting back on luxury items.

It is also important to focus on paying off high-interest debt, such as credit card balances and student loans. By reducing your debt, you can free up money for savings and investment, which can help you to weather the economic uncertainty of a recession.

Another important aspect of prioritizing savings during a recession is to develop a contingency plan. This means thinking about what you would do if you lost your job, and planning for that eventuality. This can include developing a budget that takes into account reduced income, as well as considering alternative sources of income, such as part-time work or starting a business.

It is also important to understand the role that the stock market plays during a recession. The stock market is a barometer of the overall health of the economy, and when economic activity slows, it can lead to a drop in stock prices. However, it is important to remember that stock market fluctuations are a normal part of the economic cycle, and that prices tend to recover over time.

In order to prioritize savings during a recession, it is also important to consider alternative investments, such as bonds and real estate. By diversifying your investments, you can reduce your overall risk and provide a greater degree of stability during a period of economic uncertainty.

Finally, it is important to maintain a long-term perspective when prioritizing savings during a recession. This means avoiding hasty financial decisions, such as selling all of your investments, and focusing instead on developing a long-term financial plan. By taking a calm and measured approach to your finances, you can minimize the impact of a recession and ensure a stable financial future.

In conclusion, prioritizing savings during a recession is an important step in ensuring a stable financial future. By reducing expenses, paying off debt, and diversifying investments, you can minimize the impact of a recession and weather the economic uncertainty of this challenging time. By maintaining a long-term perspective and avoiding hasty financial decisions, you can ensure that you are on track to achieving your financial goals and securing a stable financial future.

CHAPTER SIXTEEN

Develop a contingency plan

A recession is a period of economic decline that can lead to reduced consumer spending, increased unemployment, and a decline in the stock market. While these events can be unsettling, it is important to remember that a recession is a natural part of the economic cycle and that there are steps that can be taken to minimize its impact. One of the most important steps is to develop a contingency plan.

A contingency plan is a set of steps that you can take to prepare for and respond to a period of economic uncertainty. This plan should include strategies for reducing expenses, increasing income, and maintaining your financial stability, even if your income is reduced or you lose your job.

One of the first steps in developing a contingency plan is to build an emergency fund. This fund should be used to cover essential expenses, such as housing, food, and transportation, in the event that you lose your job or experience a reduction in income. It is recommended that you aim to save at least three to six months' worth of living expenses in this fund.

Another important step in developing a contingency plan is to reduce debt. This means paying off credit card balances, student loans, and other forms of high-interest debt, which can be especially burdensome during a period of economic uncertainty. By reducing your debt, you will have more money available to cover essential expenses and to invest in your future.

It is also important to diversify your investments during a recession. This means spreading your investments across different asset classes, such as stocks, bonds, and real estate, so that you are not overly exposed to any one sector of the economy. This can help to reduce your overall risk and provide a greater degree of stability during a period of economic uncertainty.

In addition to reducing debt and diversifying your investments, it is also important to cut non-essential expenses during a recession. This can include cutting back on dining out, entertainment, and travel, as well as reducing your overall spending on luxury items. By reducing your expenses, you will have more money available to save and invest, which can help you weather the economic downturn.

Another key strategy for developing a contingency plan during a recession is to increase your income. This can include taking on part-time work, starting a side business, or pursuing new job opportunities. It is also important to improve your skills and education, so that you are well-positioned to take advantage of new job opportunities when they arise.

In addition to these steps, it is also important to stay informed about the state of the economy and the stock market. This means staying up-to-date on the latest news and trends, and seeking advice from financial experts when necessary. By staying informed, you can make informed decisions about your finances and take the necessary steps to protect your financial future.

Finally, it is important to seek support from loved ones during a recession. This can include talking to friends and family about your financial concerns, and seeking advice from trusted advisors. By reaching out to others, you can build a network of support that can help you weather the economic downturn.

In conclusion, a recession can be a difficult and uncertain time, but with a well-developed contingency plan, you can minimize its impact and maintain your financial stability. By building an emergency fund, reducing debt, diversifying your investments, cutting non-essential expenses, increasing your income, staying informed, and seeking support, you can take control of your financial future and weather the economic downturn with confidence.

Focus on necessities

The impact of a recession can be felt by people from all walks of life, and it is important to have a plan in place to weather the storm. In this essay, we will explore the importance of focusing on necessities during a recession, and offer practical tips for doing so.

The first step in preparing for a recession is to understand the impact it can have on your finances. Recessions typically result in decreased consumer spending, which can lead to reduced income and increased unemployment. In order to prepare for this, it is important to build an emergency fund that can cover your essential expenses in the event of job loss or reduced income. This fund should cover necessities such as food, housing, and transportation, and should be large enough to cover your expenses for at least six months.

Another important step in preparing for a recession is to reduce debt. High-interest debt, such as credit card balances and student loans, can be especially burdensome during a period of economic uncertainty. By paying off debt, you can reduce your monthly expenses and free up money for savings and investment.

One of the best ways to focus on necessities during a recession is to cut back on non-essential expenses. This can include reducing spending on dining out, entertainment, and travel, as well as reducing your overall spending on luxury items. By cutting back on these expenses, you can free up money for savings and investment, and ensure that you have the resources you need to cover your essential expenses.

In addition to cutting back on non-essential expenses, it is also important to prioritize savings during a recession. This means setting aside a portion of your income each month for your emergency fund and other investments. By doing so, you can ensure that you have the resources you need to weather the storm and maintain your standard of living, even if your income decreases.

Another key strategy for focusing on necessities during a recession is to be proactive about your career and job security. This means improving your skills and education, networking for job opportunities, and being open to new career paths. By being proactive about your career, you can ensure that you are well-positioned to weather the storm, even if your current job is impacted by the recession.

It is also important to be adaptable during a recession. This means being open to new job opportunities, even if they are not in your current field, and being willing to relocate for work if necessary. By being adaptable, you can ensure that you have the resources you need to maintain your standard of living, even if your income decreases.

Finally, it is important to seek support from loved ones during a recession. This can include reaching out to friends and family for support and advice, and seeking the help of a financial advisor if necessary. By seeking support from those around you, you can ensure that you have the resources you need to weather the storm and maintain your standard of living.

In conclusion, focusing on necessities during a recession is a critical step in weathering the storm and maintaining your standard of living. By building an emergency fund, reducing debt, cutting back on non-essential expenses, prioritizing savings, being proactive about your career, being adaptable, and seeking support from loved ones, you can ensure that you have the resources you need to survive and thrive during a period of economic uncertainty.

CHAPTER EIGHTEEN

Take advantage of lower prices

While a recession can be a difficult time for many people, it is also an opportunity to take advantage of lower prices and improve your financial situation. By understanding the ways that you can take advantage of lower prices during a recession, you can minimize the impact of the economic downturn and position yourself for future financial success.

One of the most direct ways to take advantage of lower prices during a recession is to focus on necessities. When the economy slows down, businesses may offer discounts on essential items, such as food, clothing, and household goods. This is a great opportunity to save money on items that you need to purchase anyway, and to stock up on supplies for the future.

Another way to take advantage of lower prices during a recession is to delay big purchases. When the economy slows down, many businesses are eager to increase sales, which can lead to discounts on items such as cars, appliances, and electronics. If you have been considering making a big purchase, now may be the time to take advantage of these discounts and save money on your purchase.

In addition to taking advantage of lower prices on necessities and big-ticket items, you can also take advantage of lower prices during a recession by improving your skills and education. This can include taking courses or pursuing certifications that will increase your marketability and earning potential, as well as seeking out professional development opportunities that will help you to improve your skills and stay current with industry trends.

Another way to take advantage of lower prices during a recession is to start a business. With unemployment rates high and businesses closing, there may be opportunities to start a new business or to take advantage of lower prices on business supplies and equipment. This can be a great way to create a new source of income and to take advantage of the lower prices and increased opportunities that come with a recession.

Finally, it is important to remember that lower prices during a recession can also be a great opportunity to invest in your financial future. By taking advantage of lower prices on investments such as stocks and real estate, you can position yourself for future financial success, even during a period of economic uncertainty.

In conclusion, while a recession can be a difficult time for many people, it is also an opportunity to take advantage of lower prices and to improve your financial situation. Whether you are focused on necessities, big-ticket items, skills and education, business opportunities, or investments, taking advantage of lower prices during a recession can help you to minimize the impact of the economic downturn and to position yourself for future financial success. By understanding the ways that you can take advantage of lower prices during a recession, you can take control of your financial future and improve your overall quality of life.

CHAPTER NINETEEN

Utilize unemployment benefits

For many people, the impact of a recession can be devastating, leading to job loss, reduced income, and increased financial stress. However, there are tools available to help people weather the impact of a recession, including unemployment benefits.

Unemployment benefits are a form of government assistance provided to individuals who have lost their jobs through no fault of their own. They are designed to help people make ends meet while they search for new employment, and they can be an invaluable resource during a period of economic uncertainty.

To be eligible for unemployment benefits, you must meet certain criteria, including being actively seeking work and being able to show that you have recently been employed. You will also need to meet specific income requirements, as well as reside in the state where you are applying for benefits.

Once you have determined that you are eligible for unemployment benefits, the next step is to file a claim. This can typically be done online or in person, and you will need to provide information about your previous employment, your current circumstances, and your plans for finding new work.

In order to maximize your benefits, it is important to be proactive about your job search. This means keeping a record of all of your job search activities, including job applications, resume submissions, and interviews. You should also make sure to actively seek out new job opportunities and be open to new career paths.

It is also important to stay informed about the status of your unemployment benefits and to take advantage of any additional resources that are available, such as job training programs or career counseling services.

In addition to providing a financial safety net, unemployment benefits can also help to reduce the stress that comes with job loss. By providing a steady source of income, they can help you to focus on your job search, rather than worrying about how to pay your bills.

While unemployment benefits can be an invaluable resource during a recession, it is important to remember that they are not a permanent solution. Instead, they are designed to help you transition to a new job as quickly and smoothly as possible. This means that you should continue to actively seek new employment, even as you receive unemployment benefits.

It is also important to be mindful of the impact of unemployment benefits on your finances. While they can provide a critical source of income, they are typically less than your previous salary, and they are subject to taxes. This means that you will need to carefully manage your finances and make changes to your spending habits, in order to ensure that your benefits last as long as possible.

In conclusion, unemployment benefits are an important tool for individuals who have lost their jobs during a recession. By providing a financial safety net and reducing the stress of job loss, they can help you to weather the impact of a recession and make a smooth transition to a new job. However, it is important to be proactive about your job search and to carefully manage your finances, in order to maximize the benefits of this program.

CHAPTER TWENTY

Improve skills and education

It can be difficult to navigate the uncertain waters of a recession, but there is one key strategy that can help to minimize the impact of this economic cycle: improving your skills and education. By investing in yourself and your future, you can increase your chances of financial stability and long-term success.

One of the biggest challenges during a recession is finding work. With unemployment rates on the rise, competition for jobs can be fierce. This is why it is more important than ever to make sure that you have the skills and education that employers are looking for. This means taking the time to assess your current skills and identify areas for improvement, and then taking steps to close any skill gaps.

One of the best ways to improve your skills is by taking courses and workshops. This can be done in a number of different ways, from enrolling in a local college or university, to taking online courses or participating in community education programs. By improving your skills and education, you can increase your value to employers, making it easier to find work during a recession.

Another key aspect of improving your skills and education is staying up-to-date with industry trends and advancements. This means reading trade publications, attending industry conferences and events, and participating in professional organizations. By staying informed and engaged, you can ensure that you are always at the forefront of your industry, making you an attractive candidate for employers.

In addition to improving your skills and education, it is also important to network with others in your industry. This means building relationships with professionals in your field, and seeking out mentors who can help guide you and provide valuable advice. Networking can also help you to identify new job opportunities, and increase your chances of finding work during a recession.

Another way to invest in your future is by starting your own business. During a recession, many people are laid off from their jobs and struggle to find new employment. Starting a business can be a way to create your own job and secure your financial future. It can also provide you with greater control over your income, and the freedom to pursue your passions and interests.

Starting a business does require effort, dedication, and a willingness to take risks. However, it can be a rewarding and fulfilling experience, and a path to financial stability during a recession.

It is also important to focus on personal development during a recession. This means taking care of your physical and mental health, and finding ways to reduce stress and stay positive. This can include practicing mindfulness, exercise, and spending time with loved ones. By taking care of yourself, you can be more focused and productive, and better equipped to handle the challenges of a recession.

In conclusion, investing in yourself and your future is one of the best ways to minimize the impact of a recession. Whether you choose to improve your skills and education, network with others in your industry, or start your own business, you can increase your chances of financial stability and long-term success. By focusing on your personal growth and development, and taking a proactive approach to your career, you can navigate the uncertain waters of a recession and come out stronger on the other side.

CHAPTER TWENTY-ONE

Network for job opportunities

Recession is not the end of the world, and that there are many steps you can take to minimize its impact on your life. One of the most effective strategies for finding job opportunities during a recession is to utilize your network.

Your network is made up of people who you know, including friends, family, colleagues, and acquaintances. By tapping into your network, you can increase your chances of finding a new job, and you can also gain valuable insight into the job market and the types of positions that are available.

One of the best ways to use your network for job opportunities is to attend networking events and professional associations. These events provide a great opportunity to meet new people, make connections, and learn about job openings. You can also attend career fairs and job search workshops, which can be a great way to meet potential employers and learn about job opportunities.

In addition to attending events, you can also use your network to reach out to people who work in your field or industry. For example, you can reach out to former colleagues, classmates, or friends who work in your field and ask them about job openings or opportunities for networking. This can be especially effective if you have a strong relationship with these people and if they are in a position to help you.

Another way to use your network for job opportunities is to join online professional networks and job search sites. These sites provide a platform for connecting with other professionals in your field, and they can be a great way to learn about job openings and to connect with potential employers. For example, LinkedIn is a popular social networking site for professionals, and it provides a platform for connecting with other professionals, finding job openings, and building your online presence.

Finally, you can also use your network to learn about new job opportunities through word of mouth. For example, you can ask your friends and family members if they know of any job openings, or if they have heard of any companies that are hiring. This can be an effective way to find job opportunities, as people in your network are often willing to help you and to provide you with valuable information about the job market.

It is important to remember that networking is not a one-time event, but rather a long-term process that requires time and effort. In order to be successful, you need to be proactive, persistent, and focused on your goals. This means setting aside time to attend events, making new connections, and following up with the people you meet.

In addition to utilizing your network, there are other steps you can take to find job opportunities during a recession. For example, you can improve your skills and education, seek advice from career counselors, and seek support from loved ones. By taking a proactive and strategic approach to your job search, you can increase your chances of finding a new job and minimizing the impact of a recession on your life.

In conclusion, using your network for job opportunities is an effective way to find a new job during a recession. By attending events, reaching out to people in your field, and utilizing online professional networks, you can increase your chances of finding a new job and minimize the impact of a recession on your life.

CHAPTER TWENTY-TWO

Consider starting a business

While this can be a difficult time for many people, it can also provide a unique opportunity for those who are willing to take a risk and start a new business. In this essay, we will explore the reasons why starting a business during a recession can be a smart choice, and provide tips for those who are considering taking the leap.

One of the key benefits of starting a business during a recession is that there is often less competition. As other businesses struggle to survive, entrepreneurs who are willing to take a risk can take advantage of the opportunities that are available. This can mean lower overhead costs, less competition for customers, and greater opportunities for growth.

Another advantage of starting a business during a recession is that the cost of starting a business is often lower. This can include lower costs for supplies, lower salaries for employees, and lower costs for office space. In addition, many entrepreneurs are able to secure financing at more favorable terms during a recession, making it easier to get their business off the ground.

In order to be successful when starting a business during a recession, it is important to focus on a niche that is in high demand. This means identifying a product or service that is in high demand, and that is not easily available from other businesses. For example, businesses that focus on providing essential goods and services, such as food and healthcare, are likely to be more successful during a recession than those that focus on luxury items.

Another key factor to consider when starting a business during a recession is to focus on providing excellent customer service. This means providing a high-quality product or service, and going the extra mile to ensure that your customers are satisfied. By focusing on customer service, you can differentiate yourself from your competition, and build a loyal customer base that will help your business to succeed.

Starting a business during a recession also requires a willingness to adapt to changing circumstances. This means being flexible and open to new ideas, and being willing to change your approach as the market evolves. This can mean shifting your focus to new products or services, or changing your business model to better meet the needs of your customers.

In addition to being adaptable, it is also important to have a strong work ethic when starting a business during a recession. This means putting in the time and effort to build your business, and being persistent in the face of challenges and obstacles. With a strong work ethic, you can turn your business into a success, even during a period of economic uncertainty.

Finally, it is important to seek out support and advice from others when starting a business during a recession. This can include seeking the advice of business mentors, networking with other entrepreneurs, and joining business organizations or groups. With the right support and advice, you can gain the knowledge and skills you need to succeed, and turn your business into a success.

In conclusion, starting a business during a recession can be a smart choice for those who are willing to take a risk and invest in their future. With a focus on providing essential goods and services, excellent customer service, and adaptability, you can turn your business into a success, even during a period of economic uncertainty. By seeking out support and advice from others, and having a strong work ethic, you can build a business that will last for many years to come.

CHAPTER TWENTY-THREE

Be proactive about job security

While a recession can be a difficult time for workers, it is possible to take proactive steps to protect your job and maintain your standard of living. In this essay, we will explore some of the strategies you can use to be proactive about job security during a recession.

One of the best ways to protect your job during a recession is to focus on your skills and education. This means investing time and resources into developing new skills, learning new technologies, and keeping up-to-date with industry trends. By continuously improving your skills, you can increase your value to your employer and reduce the risk of losing your job.

Another key strategy for protecting your job during a recession is to be proactive about your work schedule. This means being punctual, reliable, and consistently delivering high-quality work. By demonstrating your commitment to your job and your employer, you can increase your chances of retaining your position during a period of economic uncertainty.

It is also important to be open to new job opportunities during a recession. This means being willing to consider part-time work, freelance opportunities, or alternative forms of employment. By keeping your options open, you can increase your chances of finding new job opportunities in the event that you lose your current position.

Networking is another important strategy for protecting your job during a recession. This means connecting with other professionals in your industry, participating in industry events, and staying informed about job openings and industry trends. By building a strong network, you can increase your chances of being recommended for new job opportunities, and you can also gain valuable insights into the state of the job market.

In order to be proactive about job security during a recession, it is also important to be adaptable. This means being flexible in your job search and being willing to consider new industries, job functions, and locations. By being adaptable, you can increase your chances of finding new job opportunities and protecting your standard of living.

Finally, it is important to develop a contingency plan for the event that you lose your job during a recession. This can include reducing expenses, cutting back on non-essential spending, and seeking support from friends and family. By having a plan in place, you can reduce the stress and uncertainty that comes with job loss, and you can ensure that you are able to maintain your standard of living.

In conclusion, a recession can be a difficult time for workers, but it is possible to protect your job and maintain your standard of living by taking proactive steps. This includes focusing on your skills and education, being proactive about your work schedule, being open to new job opportunities, networking, being adaptable, and developing a contingency plan. By taking these steps, you can increase your chances of retaining your job and protecting your financial future during a period of economic uncertainty.

CHAPTER TWENTY-FOUR

Delay retirement savings

Recession is a natural part of the economic cycle and can have a significant impact on the stock market, which is often considered a barometer of the overall health of the economy. During a recession, it can be tempting to panic and withdraw savings from retirement accounts, but this is often not a wise financial decision. Instead, it is often better to delay retirement savings during a recession, in order to protect your financial future and minimize the impact of the economic downturn.

One of the key reasons why it is a good idea to delay retirement savings during a recession is that the stock market is typically volatile during this time. This means that prices can fluctuate significantly, and it can be difficult to predict what will happen in the future. If you withdraw your savings from the stock market during a period of declining prices, you may end up selling at the bottom of the market and missing out on the eventual rebound.

Another reason why it is important to delay retirement savings during a recession is that this can help you to weather the economic downturn. During a recession, unemployment is often high, and many people experience a reduction in income. By delaying retirement savings, you can free up money to cover essential expenses, such as food, housing, and transportation, and reduce the stress that comes with financial uncertainty.

In addition to helping you to weather the economic downturn, delaying retirement savings during a recession can also help you to maximize your long-term savings. This is because the stock market tends to recover over time, and by delaying your retirement savings, you can take advantage of the eventual rebound in prices. This can help you to build a more substantial nest egg for retirement, and reduce your dependence on Social Security and other forms of government support.

However, it is important to understand that delaying retirement savings during a recession is not a one-size-fits-all solution, and that the right strategy will depend on your individual financial situation. For example, if you are close to retirement age, you may need to consider alternative strategies, such as reducing your spending or finding part-time work, in order to maintain your standard of living.

If you are still many years away from retirement, it may be possible to delay your savings for a few years, and then ramp up your contributions once the economy has recovered. This will help you to avoid having to withdraw savings from the stock market during a period of declining prices, and it can also help you to take advantage of the eventual rebound in prices.

In conclusion, delaying retirement savings during a recession can be a prudent financial decision, helping you to weather the economic downturn and maximizing your long-term savings. However, it is important to understand that this is not a one-size-fits-all solution, and that the right strategy will depend on your individual financial situation.

If you are unsure about the best approach for your situation, it may be helpful to speak with a financial advisor, who can provide guidance and help you to make informed decisions about your retirement savings.

CHAPTER TWENTY-FIVE

Stay open to new job opportunities

While this can be a challenging time for you, it is important to remain open to new job opportunities in order to weather the storm.

One of the first things to keep in mind during a recession is that the job market is constantly changing. This means that new job opportunities may arise, even during a period of economic uncertainty. It is important to remain vigilant and be proactive in seeking out new job opportunities, as this can increase your chances of finding employment.

One of the best ways to stay informed about new job opportunities is to network. This means reaching out to friends, family members, and former colleagues to ask about any job openings or opportunities that may be available. You can also attend job fairs, participate in professional organizations, and use social media to connect with potential employers.

It is also important to improve your skills and education during a recession, as this can make you a more attractive candidate for new job opportunities. This can involve taking courses or certifications, or seeking out on-the-job training. By investing in yourself and your skills, you can increase your competitiveness in the job market and improve your chances of finding employment.

Another important strategy for finding new job opportunities during a recession is to be adaptable. This means being open to new industries, job roles, or locations, even if they are outside of your comfort zone. By being open to new opportunities, you can increase your chances of finding a job that fits your skills and interests.

It is also important to consider relocating for work during a recession, as this can open up new job opportunities in other parts of the country. This may involve moving to a different city or state, but the benefits of increased job opportunities and a better quality of life can make it worth the effort.

In addition to being proactive and adaptable, it is also important to have a positive attitude during a recession. This means maintaining a sense of optimism and focusing on the opportunities that are available, rather than the challenges. This can be a difficult mindset to maintain during a period of economic uncertainty, but it is essential for staying motivated and finding new job opportunities.

Finally, it is important to seek support from loved ones during a recession, as this can help to reduce stress and provide a sense of comfort during a challenging time. Whether it is through emotional support, financial assistance, or simply being there to listen, the support of friends and family can make all the difference during a period of economic uncertainty.

In conclusion, staying open to new job opportunities during a recession can be a key strategy for weathering the storm. By being proactive, adaptable, positive, and seeking support, you can increase your chances of finding new employment and maintaining your financial stability during a period of economic uncertainty.

CHAPTER TWENTY-SIX

Be adaptable

It is important to approach the situation with a sense of adaptability and resilience. By being adaptable and making smart financial decisions, it is possible to minimize the impact of a recession and come out on the other side stronger and more financially secure.

One of the most important strategies for surviving and thriving during a recession is to be proactive about job security. This means taking steps to improve your skills, seeking out new job opportunities, and staying informed about the job market. If you are working in an industry that is particularly vulnerable to recession, it may be worth considering a career change or seeking out new job opportunities in industries that are more recession-proof.

Another important strategy for surviving and thriving during a recession is to be open to new job opportunities. This means being willing to relocate, to work in a different industry, or to take on a part-time job if necessary. By being open to new opportunities, you can increase your chances of finding work and maintaining your standard of living during a difficult time.

It is also important to prioritize savings during a recession. This means cutting back on non-essential expenses and putting aside as much money as possible for your emergency fund. A strong emergency fund will help you to weather the storm of unemployment or reduced income, and it will provide you with a sense of financial security during a difficult time.

One of the best ways to minimize the impact of a recession is to develop a contingency plan. This means thinking ahead and considering what you would do if you lost your job or experienced a reduction in income. This might include cutting back on expenses, seeking out new job opportunities, or exploring alternative sources of income. By having a contingency plan in place, you will be better prepared to handle the challenges of a recession and minimize the impact on your financial well-being.

In addition to being adaptable and proactive about job security, it is also important to maintain a long-term perspective during a recession. This means focusing on your financial goals and avoiding making hasty financial decisions. For example, it is not always a good idea to sell all of your investments during a period of market volatility, as prices are likely to recover over time. By taking a long-term perspective and avoiding impulsive financial decisions, you can minimize the impact of a recession on your finances and come out on the other side in a stronger position.

Another important strategy for surviving and thriving during a recession is to seek out advice from financial experts. This might include consulting with a financial advisor, reading financial books and articles, or attending financial seminars. By seeking out expert advice, you can gain a better understanding of the economic landscape and make informed decisions about your finances.

Finally, it is important to seek support from loved ones during a recession. Whether it is a supportive partner, a trusted friend, or a caring family member, having a support network can help you to weather the challenges of a recession and maintain a positive outlook.

In conclusion, a recession can be a difficult time for everyone, but by being adaptable, proactive, and long-term focused, it is possible to minimize the impact and come out on the other side stronger and more financially secure. By developing a contingency plan, seeking out expert advice, and seeking support from loved ones, you can navigate the challenges of a recession and emerge in a better position on the other side.

CHAPTER TWENTY-SEVEN

Consider relocating for work

During recession, calculate the opportunity for people to re-evaluate their career goals and to make changes that can improve their long-term financial stability. One option to consider during a recession is relocating for work.

Relocating for work can be a difficult decision, as it often involves leaving behind familiar communities, friends, and family. However, it can also provide many benefits, including improved job opportunities, higher salaries, and access to new career paths. During a recession, relocating can be especially attractive, as it can provide an escape from a challenging job market and a chance to take advantage of new opportunities.

One of the biggest advantages of relocating for work is improved job opportunities. During a recession, many companies may be downsizing or closing, making it difficult to find work in certain regions. By relocating to areas with a stronger economy, you may be able to find better job prospects and secure a more stable financial future.

In addition to improved job opportunities, relocating for work can also provide access to higher salaries. This can be especially important during a recession, when many people are facing pay cuts or reduced hours. By moving to an area with a strong economy, you may be able to find a job that pays more than your current job, helping you to secure a stronger financial future.

Relocating for work can also provide an opportunity to explore new career paths. By moving to a new area, you may be exposed to new industries, technologies, and job opportunities that you may not have had access to in your current location. This can be a great opportunity to broaden your skill set and to explore new career paths that may provide more stability and growth opportunities in the future.

Another advantage of relocating for work is access to new communities and a higher quality of life. By moving to a new area, you may be able to experience a new culture, a better quality of life, and a stronger sense of community. This can be especially important during a recession, when many people are feeling isolated and stressed about their financial future.

While relocating for work can provide many benefits, it is important to approach this decision carefully and to consider the potential challenges. For example, relocating can be expensive, as you will need to cover the costs of moving, housing, and transportation. Additionally, you will need to adjust to a new community and to new ways of living, which can be difficult and stressful.

To ensure a successful relocation, it is important to research potential destinations carefully and to consider factors such as the local economy, job prospects, and quality of life. You should also talk to friends and family about your plans, as they can provide valuable support and advice during this transition.

Additionally, it is important to prepare for the financial challenges of relocating, such as the cost of housing, transportation, and moving expenses. You may need to save money, reduce your spending, or take on additional debt in order to cover these costs. It is also important to have a plan for finding a job in your new location, such as networking with local professionals, applying for jobs online, and seeking advice from career counselors.

In conclusion, relocating for work can be a great opportunity during a recession, providing improved job prospects, higher salaries, and access to new career paths. However, it is important to approach this decision carefully and to consider the potential challenges, such as the cost of relocating, the difficulty of adjusting to a new community, and the need to find a new job. By researching potential destinations carefully, preparing for the financial challenges of rel

CHAPTER TWENTY-EIGHT

Seek advice from financial experts

While it is natural to feel overwhelmed, it is important to remember that there is help available. Seeking advice from financial experts can be a valuable step in navigating the challenges of a recession and protecting your financial future.

One of the primary reasons to seek advice from financial experts during a recession is to better understand the impact of economic events on your finances. Financial experts can provide insight into the broader economic trends that are driving the recession, as well as the specific impact that these trends are having on your personal financial situation. This information can help you to make informed decisions about your investments, spending, and overall financial strategy.

Another important reason to seek financial advice during a recession is to ensure that your investments are well-diversified. A financial expert can help you to understand the different asset classes, such as stocks, bonds, and real estate, and the role that each one plays in your overall investment strategy. They can also help you to assess your risk tolerance and develop a well-diversified portfolio that can weather the ups and downs of the market.

Financial experts can also provide guidance on how to reduce debt and increase savings during a recession. This can include tips on reducing expenses, finding additional sources of income, and developing a budget that prioritizes savings and debt reduction. A financial expert can also help you to understand the various types of debt, such as credit card debt and student loans, and the best strategies for reducing each one.

It is also important to seek financial advice during a recession if you are considering major financial decisions, such as buying a home, starting a business, or retiring. A financial expert can help you to understand the potential impact of these decisions on your overall financial health, and provide guidance on the best strategies for achieving your financial goals.

So, how do you go about seeking advice from a financial expert during a recession? One of the first steps is to identify your specific needs and goals. This will help you to determine the type of financial expert who is best equipped to help you, whether it is a financial planner, a stockbroker, or a tax professional.

Once you have identified your specific needs, you can start your search for a financial expert. There are many resources available, including financial planning organizations, professional associations, and online directories. You can also ask for recommendations from friends and family, or reach out to financial experts directly through their websites or social media platforms.

When choosing a financial expert, it is important to consider their qualifications, experience, and reputation. You can check their credentials through professional organizations, and research their track record and experience through online resources such as customer reviews and testimonials.

It is also important to find a financial expert who you are comfortable working with and who shares your values and goals. You will be working with this person over an extended period of time, so it is important to establish a good working relationship and to feel confident in their ability to help you achieve your financial goals.

Finally, be prepared to be an active participant in the process. This means being open to the advice and guidance provided by the financial expert, and being proactive about taking the steps necessary to improve your financial situation. This may involve making difficult decisions, such as reducing expenses or increasing savings, but with the support and guidance of a financial expert, you can be confident in your ability to weather the challenges of a recession and secure your financial future.

In conclusion, seeking advice from financial experts during a recession can be a valuable step in protecting

CHAPTER TWENTY-NINE

Keep perspective on market fluctuations

It is natural to be concerned about the impact of a recession, it is important to keep a long-term perspective and avoid panicking during periods of market fluctuations.

The stock market is a barometer of the overall health of the economy, and when economic activity slows, it can lead to a drop in stock prices. This can be a frightening experience for those who have invested their savings in the stock market, and it can lead to a feeling of helplessness. However, it is important to remember that stock market fluctuations are a normal part of the economic cycle and that prices tend to recover over time.

In order to keep a long-term perspective during a recession, it is important to understand the underlying factors that are driving the economy. For example, the unemployment rate, consumer spending, and the performance of key industries are all important indicators of the health of the economy. When these factors start to decline, it can indicate that a recession is on the horizon, which can lead to a decrease in stock prices.

However, it is important to remember that the stock market is a forward-looking indicator and that it tends to anticipate future economic activity. This means that a drop in stock prices can actually be a sign that the economy is about to recover, and that prices will eventually start to rise again.

In addition to keeping a long-term perspective, it is also important to avoid making hasty financial decisions during a period of market fluctuations. For example, selling all of your investments during a market downturn can be a mistake, as it can lock in your losses and prevent you from benefiting from the eventual recovery.

Instead, it is important to maintain a balanced investment portfolio and to stick to your long-term financial plan, even during periods of market volatility. This means focusing on your goals, such as saving for retirement, and avoiding the temptation to make short-term decisions based on fear or emotion.

Another important strategy for keeping perspective on market fluctuations during a recession is to seek advice from financial experts. This can help you to understand the underlying factors driving the economy and to make informed decisions about your investments.

It is also important to remember that diversifying your investments is a key strategy for minimizing your risk during a recession. This means spreading your investments across different asset classes, such as stocks, bonds, and real estate, so that you are not overly exposed to any one sector of the economy. This can help to reduce your overall risk and provide a greater degree of stability during a period of economic uncertainty.

Finally, it is important to stay informed about current events and to understand the impact that they may have on the stock market. For example, political events such as elections or international tensions can cause significant fluctuations in stock prices, and it is important to be aware of these events in order to make informed decisions about your investments.

In conclusion, keeping a long-term perspective and avoiding hasty financial decisions are key strategies for minimizing the impact of market fluctuations during a recession. By focusing on your goals, seeking advice from financial experts, and staying informed about current events, you can navigate the challenges of a recession with confidence and maintain your financial stability over the long-term.

CHAPTER THIRTY

Avoid making hasty financial decisions

It can be a challenging time for everyone, and it can be tempting to make hasty financial decisions in an effort to protect your finances. However, it is important to resist the urge to make impulsive moves, as these decisions can often do more harm than good. Instead, it is important to take a calm and measured approach to your finances during a recession, in order to minimize the impact and help secure your financial future.

One of the biggest mistakes people make during a recession is to sell all of their investments in a panic. This can be a tempting move, especially if you are worried about losing money in the stock market. However, it is important to remember that the stock market is a forward-looking indicator, and that prices tend to recover over time. By selling all of your investments, you risk missing out on the potential for future growth, and you could end up losing money in the long run.

Another common mistake during a recession is to withdraw money from retirement accounts. This can be a tempting move, especially if you are facing financial hardship, but it can have serious consequences.

Withdrawing money from a retirement account before retirement age can result in penalties, taxes, and a reduction in the amount of money you will have available in retirement.

It is also important to avoid making hasty decisions about your job during a recession. While it may be tempting to take the first job offer that comes your way, even if it pays less or is in a different field, it is important to think carefully about your long-term career goals and the impact that this decision could have on your future earnings potential.

Another important strategy for avoiding hasty financial decisions during a recession is to focus on paying down debt. This can help to reduce your overall financial stress and improve your overall financial health. You can also consider consolidating your debt, which can reduce your monthly payments and make it easier to manage your finances.

It is also important to maintain a long-term perspective during a recession. While it can be tempting to focus solely on the short-term, it is important to think about your financial future and the impact that your decisions today will have on your long-term financial health. This means considering the potential consequences of any financial decisions, and making choices that will help you to achieve your long-term financial goals.

In addition to avoiding hasty financial decisions, it is also important to seek advice from financial experts during a recession. This can include working with a financial advisor, seeking advice from a financial planner, or reading books and articles about personal finance. Having a good understanding of the economic cycle, the stock market, and personal finance can help you to make informed decisions and protect your financial future.

Finally, it is important to focus on maintaining a healthy lifestyle during a recession. This can include eating a balanced diet, getting regular exercise, and getting adequate sleep. Taking care of yourself can help you to maintain a positive outlook and reduce the stress that comes with financial uncertainty.

In conclusion, making hasty financial decisions during a recession can have serious consequences for your financial future. Instead, it is important to take a calm and measured approach, focusing on maintaining a long-term perspective, seeking advice from financial experts, and taking care of your overall health and wellbeing. By taking these steps, you can help to minimize the impact of a recession on your finances.

CHAPTER THIRTY-ONE

Seek support from loved ones

The impact of a recession can be felt throughout society, causing people to feel anxious and worried about their financial future. While it is natural to feel concerned about the impact of a recession, it is important to remember that we are not alone and that there is support available. One of the most important sources of support during a recession is the people we love.

Loved ones can provide a great deal of comfort and support during a recession. They can listen to our concerns, offer practical advice, and provide emotional support as we navigate this challenging time. It is important to reach out to loved ones and to be open about our feelings and concerns, rather than trying to deal with everything on our own. This can help us to feel less isolated and more connected to the people who matter most to us.

In addition to providing emotional support, loved ones can also offer practical help during a recession. For example, family members or friends may be able to help with job searching, or offer to help with childcare or transportation while we look for work. This type of support can be incredibly valuable during a period of financial uncertainty, as it can help us to stay focused on our goals and to maintain our standard of living.

Another important source of support during a recession is the larger community. Joining a support group or participating in community events can help us to connect with others who are facing similar challenges. This can provide a sense of belonging and can help us to feel less isolated as we navigate this difficult time.

In addition to seeking support from loved ones and the community, it is also important to take steps to care for our mental and emotional health during a recession. This may mean seeking professional help if we are struggling with anxiety or depression, or finding ways to relax and de-stress, such as through exercise, meditation, or hobbies.

Finally, it is important to remember that recessions are a natural part of the economic cycle, and that they are not permanent. While it may be challenging in the short term, the economy has a tendency to recover over time, and it is important to maintain a long-term perspective and to focus on our goals.

In conclusion, a recession can be a challenging time for many people, but it is important to remember that we are not alone and that there is support available. Seeking support from loved ones, participating in community events, and taking steps to care for our mental and emotional health can all help us to navigate this difficult time and to emerge stronger on the other side. By taking a calm and measured approach, we can minimize the impact of a recession and ensure a brighter financial future for ourselves and our loved ones.

Conclusion

In conclusion, while a recession can be a difficult and uncertain time, it is important to approach the situation with a calm and measured understanding of the facts. By focusing on developing a solid financial plan, reducing debt, and diversifying investments, it is possible to escape the negative impacts of a recession and maintain a stable financial future.

One of the most important steps you can take is to build an emergency fund, which will help you to cover essential expenses in the event of job loss or reduced income. It is also important to reduce debt and focus on cutting non-essential expenses, so that you can free up money for savings and investment.

Diversifying your investments is another key strategy for escaping the impacts of a recession. This means spreading your investments across different asset classes, so that you are not overly exposed to any one sector of the economy. By doing so, you can reduce your overall risk and provide a greater degree of stability during a period of economic uncertainty.

Finally, it is important to stay informed about the current economic situation and to avoid panicking in the face of stock market fluctuations and other events. By approaching the situation with a long-term perspective, you can avoid making hasty financial decisions and ensure that your financial future is secure, even during a period of economic uncertainty.

In summary, while a recession can be a difficult time, it is possible to escape its negative impacts by developing a solid financial plan, reducing debt, diversifying investments, and staying informed and proactive. With these steps, you can maintain a stable financial future and navigate the uncertain waters of a recession with confidence.

www.ingramcontent.com/pod-product-compliance
Lightning Source LLC
Chambersburg PA
CBHW021115130726
47988CB00003B/1038